Eczema Diet Cookbook

100 Delicious Recipes to

Manage your

Eczema Inflammation

Paul Morgan

NORTHERN PRESS
PUBLISHING COMPANY

ISBN-13: 978-1546757191

ISBN-10: 1546757198

Published by Northern Press Inc.

Contents

Delicious Crepes...5

Buckwheat Pancakes with Bananas..............6

Chia Quinoa Porridge.. 8

Avocado Toast with Egg...................................8

Breakfast wrap...9

Wholesome Omelet...9

Fluffy Blueberry Waffles.................................10

Citrus Fruity Cocktail......................................12

Pineapple Smoothie..12

Flavoured Oatmeal...13

Multigrain Pancakes...14

Breakfast Bowl..15

Moist Carrot Bread..16

Healthy Berry Smoothie..................................17

Creamy Millet Porridge...................................17

Healthy Baked Oatmeal.................................18

Sweet Pineapple Muffins................................19

Colorful Omelet...20

Apple Salad Breakfast....................................22

Super Food Salad...24

Creamy Spinach Soup.....................................25

Savory Beets Soup..25

Tempting Zucchini..26

Sautéed Asparagus..28

Kale Salad...28

Herbed Chicken...29

10 Smoothie Recipes......................................30

Chicken Kebobs...34

Gourmet Stuffed Bell Peppers......................35

Savory Meatballs with Salad.........................36

Chicken Soup..38

Omega-3 Rich Burgers....................................39

Easy Baked Chicken Tenders........................40

Easy Scallops & Zucchini................................41

Chicken Stir Fry...43

Chicken Tacos with Avocado Salsa.............44

BBQ Tuna Fritters...45

Mandarin Chicken Salad Pasta....................46

Shrimp and Pineapple Ceviche....................48

Green Bean and Potato Salad......................49

California Sandwich...50

Shrimp Noodle Soup.......................................51

Sweet Potato Fries...52

Romaine Rice Tuna Salad..............................53

Millet-Stuffed Peppers....................................54

Fabulous Chicken and Sweet Potatoes........56

Family Lentil Soup..57

Savory Trout..58

Easy Scallops & Zucchini................................60

Smoky Steak with Salsa..................................61

Nutritious Salmon Salad.................................62

Veggie Stew with Dumpling............................63

Turkey Pasta..64

Roasted Bell Pepper and Olive Pizza.............66

Yummy Lasagna......................................67

Spicy Chicken Chili...................................68

Burgers with Mushrooms and Radicchio.......69

Healthy Chicken Burritos...............................70

Lemon Asparagus Risotto............................71

Baked Parmesan Fish...................................72

Broccoli and Garlic Pasta............................74

Crunchy Chickpeas...................................74

Apple Cinnamon Pork chops........................75

Pork Chops with Honey Garlic Sauce...........75

Chicken and Sprouts Stir-fry..........................76

Creamy Ham Penne.....................................78

Baked Potato & Broccoli Soup......................79

Spaghetti and Meatballs...............................80

Baked Tortilla Chips.....................................83

Peanut Butter Nuggets..................................83

Fast Snack Wraps.....................................84

Cinnamon Chips with Fruit Salsa...................86

Grape and Avocado Salsa...........................87

Healthy Granola Bars...................................88

Spiced Sweet Roasted Red Pepper
Hummus...90

Balsamic Bruschetta.....................................92

Baked Kale Chips..94

Healthy Peanut Butter Fruit Dip.....................94

Healthy Soufflé..96

Baked Rice Pudding.....................................97

Blueberry Pudding..98

Kids Favorite Mousse..................................100

Glazed banana..101

Instant Frozen treat.....................................101

Fruity Ice Cream...102

70-Calorie Brownies...................................104

Fall-Time Custard.......................................105

Cocoa-Nut Bananas...................................106

Almond Strawberry Chia Seed Pudding.....108

Banana Chia Pudding.................................108

Mouth-Watering Fudge...............................109

Blueberries with Lemon Cream...................110

Let's Get Cooking!

Managing your eczema by avoiding foods and maintaining a healthy diet can be tough. Many of the recipes from this cookbook are influenced by anti-inflammation and Mediterranean diets because of their abundance of healthy ingredients.

Staying away from processed foods and fast foods will ensure eczema control and overall good health and you will find plenty of healthy recipes in this cookbook.

Fruits, vegetables, whole foods, omega-fatty foods are all examples of foods that are a staple in your diet to manage eczema inflammation.

So, let's get started!

BREAKFAST RECIPES

Delicious Crepes

Servings | 8

Per Serving

Calories | 120

Protein | 7g

Carbohydrates | 20g

Fat | 2g

1 1/3 cups chickpea flour

¼ teaspoon red chili powder

½ teaspoon grated ginger

1 cup cilantro leaves, chopped

1 green chilli, chopped, seeded

1 cup water

> Combine the chili powder, flour, and a pinch of salt in a bowl. Mix well. Put in the cilantro, ginger and green chili, combine well. Pour water and mix until becomes smooth. Cover the mixture for 30-120 mins.

> Put cooking spray on a skillet and heat to medium heat. Pour the mixture in and tilt pan to spread evenly. Cook 10-15 second on each side.

Buckwheat Pancakes with Bananas

Servings | 2

Per Serving

Calories | 543

Protein | 10g

Carbohydrates |91g

Fat | 19g

2 tablespoons potato starch

1 tablespoon brown sugar

1 cup buckwheat flour

2 large bananas, sliced

1 cup rice milk

2 tablespoons canola oil

1 teaspoon baking powder

½ teaspoon salt

Vegetable cooking spray, frying

Brown rice syrup

> Mix all dry ingredients into a bowl, stir well until combined whilst adding the oil and rice milk. If batter becomes too thick, add water. Preheat skillet over medium heat. Spray skillet with the cooking spray

> Using a ladle spill batter to the size your desire. Cook with medium heat until bubbles begin showing. Turn over pancake and cook until dense. Repeat until all the batter has been used. Serve with slices of banana on top and drizzled brown rice syrup.

Chia Quinoa Porridge

Servings | 2

Per Serving

Calories | 491

Protein | 14g

Carbohydrates |67g

Fat | 20g

1 tablespoon chia seeds

2 cups quinoa, cooked

1 cup blueberries

¼ cup walnuts, roasted

½ teaspoon cinnamon

2 tsp raw honey

1 cup cashew milk, thick

> Mix the cashew milk and quinoa in a pan, warm up on medium-low heat.

> Mix in the cinnamon, walnuts and blueberries until all are proportionally warm. Serve immediately in bowls

Avocado toast with Egg

Servings | 1

Per Serving

Calories |260

Protein | 9g

Carbohydrates |18g

Fat | 17g

½ of an avocado

Red pepper flakes

1 slice gluten free bread, toasted

1 ½ teaspoon ghee

Handful spinach

1 egg, scrambled

> Once you've toasted your bread top it with ghee. Put the avocado all over the bread, and then put the spinach over top.

> place the cooked egg on top of everything. Put on a bit of pepper flakes. (Add an additional slice of bread to create a sandwich)

Breakfast Wrap

Servings | 2

Per Serving

Calories | 491

Protein | 14g

Carbohydrates | 67g

Fat | 20g

2 tablespoons green bell pepper, chopped

2 tablespoons red onion, chopped

¾ cup liquid egg substitute

1 (10") whole wheat flour tortilla

> Spray a skillet with cooking spray over medium heat. Add in the veggies and cook until soft. Place in egg substitute and stir until fully cooked.

> Using a spoon put the mixture into a tortilla and roll it up to serve!

Wholesome Omelet

Servings | 1

Per Serving

Calories | 305

Protein | 13g

Carbohydrates | 22g

Fat | 19g

2 tsp coconut oil   2 large eggs

¼ tsp cinnamon   1/8 tsp nutmeg

1 tsp raw honey   pinch of salt

1/8 tsp vanilla extract

½ of cored and thinly sliced green apple

> Melt 1 tsp of oil in frying pan on medium heat, put in apple slices and put cinnamon and nutmeg over top. Cook for 5 minutes flipping 1 time in center.

> Add vanilla, eggs and salt in bowl, mix till fluffy. Add remaining oil in pan, let it melt. Add egg mix over apple slices equally. Cook for 5 minutes. Fold omelet, serve immediately

Fluffy Blueberry Waffles

Servings | 5 (1 serving: 1 waffle)

Per Serving

Calories | 274

Protein | 5g

Carbohydrates | 40g

Fat | 8g

2 eggs

2 tablespoons honey

¼ cup potato starch

2/3 cup blueberries

¾ cup unsweetened almond milk

1 teaspoon apple cider vinegar

1 teaspoon baking powder

2 tablespoons fresh lemon juice

¾ cup vanilla extract

¼ cup almond meal

2 tablespoons tapioca flour

1 teaspoon grated lemon zest

¾ cup brown rice flour

Pinch of salt

2 tablespoons melted coconut oil

> Heat a waffle iron and grease it. Mix the vinegar and milk in a bowl and set aside for a couple minutes.

> Add lemon juice, lemon zest, eggs, vanilla extract, coconut oil, and honey and beat until well mixed. In a different bowl mix together all other ingredients except for the blueberries. Add egg mixture in flour mixture and mix very well.

> In the waffle iron add the mix and cook for around 5 minutes. Rinse and repeat for left over mixture.

Citrus Fruity Cocktail

Servings | 2

Per Serving

Calories | 217

Protein | 2g

Carbohydrates | 40g

Fat | 4g

1 cup chopped frozen mango, peeled

1 cup frozen pineapple, chopped

1 peeled large frozen banana, sliced

½ cup fresh orange juice

1 teaspoon fresh lemon juice

1 cup water

1 tablespoon melted coconut oil

> Add all the ingredients into a blender, except for the coconut oil, blend till smooth. While blending, slowly add in coconut oil until creamy. Serves 2 glasses

Pineapple Smoothie

Servings | 2

Per Serving

Calories | 275

Protein | 5g

Carbohydrates | 61g

Fat | 4g

2 cups frozen pineapple, chopped

2 oranges, peeled and seeded

½ teaspoon fresh ginger, chopped

1 large frozen banana, sliced and peeled

1 teaspoon ground turmeric

2 cups unsweetened almond milk

> Pour all ingredients into a high powered blender and mix until smooth. Serve immediately.

Flavoured Oatmeal

Servings | 2

Per Serving

Calories | 285

Protein | 7g

Carbohydrates |41g

Fat | 11g

1 ½ cups unsweetened almond milk

1 cup gluten-free quick cooking oats

1 tbsp honey

½ teaspoon ground cinnamon

¾ teaspoon ground turmeric

¼ teaspoon ground ginger

¼ teaspoon ground turmeric

½ teaspoon vanilla extract

2 tablespoons blackberries

2 tablespoons pecans, chopped

> Microwave the milk and oats together in a bowl for 1 minute. Mix in the honey, extract and spices.

> Microwave an addition 2 minutes mixing half way through. Serve immediately topped with pecans and blueberries

Multigrain Pancakes

Servings | 4

Per Serving

Calories | 120

Protein | 6g

Carbohydrates | 23g

Fat | 0.5g

¼ cup whole wheat flour

¼ cup all-purpose flour

¼ cup rolled oats

¼ cup cornmeal

2 teaspoon granular no-calorie sucralose sweetener

½ teaspoon salt

1 teaspoon baking powder

½ teaspoon cinnamon

2 egg whites

2 tablespoons plain non fat yogurt

2 tablespoons skim milk

2 tablespoons water

> Stir together in a bowl the whole wheat flour, cornmeal, oats, all-purpose flour, salt, sweetener, baking soda, baking powder and cinnamon.

> In a different bowl whisk together the eggs, yogurt, milk, water. Pour the wet ingredients into the dry and mix until moistened.

> Heat a skillet over medium heat and coat with cooking spray. Pour about 1/3 cup of batter per pancake on the skillet. Cook until bubbles form and flip to other side, cook until browned.

Breakfast Bowl

Servings | 4

Per Serving

Calories | 200

Protein | 4g

Carbohydrates | 24g

Fat | 4g

2 cups unsweetened almond milk

2 green apples, cored, peeled, grated

3 tablespoons almonds, chopped, divided

3 tablespoons pecans, chopped, divided

2 tablespoons sunflower seeds

2 tablespoons pumpkin seeds

1 tablespoon honey

¼ teaspoon cinnamon

½ teaspoon vanilla extract

1 banana, peeled, sliced

¼ cup blueberries

> Combine together apple, almond milk, 1 tbsp pecans, 1 tbsp almonds, pumpkin seeds, sunflower seeds, vanilla extract, honey, and cinnamon in a large pan on medium heat.

> Cook for 5 minutes stirring often. Once serve into bowls top with remaining banana, nuts, and blueberries

Moist Carrot Bread

Servings | 10

Per Serving

Calories | 260

Protein | 6g

Carbohydrates | 24g

Fat | 18g

1 cup almond flour, blanched

¼ cup tapioca flour

1 teaspoon coconut flour

½ teaspoon baking powder

½ teaspoon baking soda

1 tsp ground turmeric

1 tsp ground cinnamon

1/8 teaspoon ground cloves

1/8 teaspoon ground nutmeg

½ teaspoon salt

1/3 cup melted coconut oil

2 tablespoons almond butter

2/3 cup coconut sugar

2 organic eggs

1 cup grated and peeled carrot

½ teaspoon grated fresh ginger

½ cup chopped walnuts

¼ cup raisins

> Preheat oven 350 degrees. Grease 9 x 5 inch loaf pan. Combine flours, spices, baking soda and powder, and salt.

> In a different bowl, put in almond butter, oil, and sugar and mix well. Put in the remaining ingredients. Put the mixture into loaf pan evenly.

> Bake around 45-50 minutes. Remove bread pan from oven and cool on wire rack for 10 minutes. Cut bread into desired slice sizes.

Healthy Berry Smoothie

Servings | 2

Per Serving

Calories | 112

Protein | 1g

Carbohydrates | 25g

Fat | 2g

1 cup unsweetened raspberries

¾ cup chilled unsweetened almond milk

¼ cup frozen pitted unsweetened cherries

1 ½ tablespoons honey

2 teaspoons grated ginger

1 teaspoon ground flaxseed

2 teaspoons fresh lemon juice

> Combine all ingredients into a blender until fully smooth. Serve in 2 glasses.

Creamy Millet Porridge

1 tablespoon coconut oil

1 teaspoon ground ginger

2 teaspoons cinnamon

½ teaspoon ground cloves

1 ½ cups millet, grounded

3 cups unsweetened almond milk

2 tablespoons honey

Servings | 4

Per Serving

Calories | 260

Protein | 9g

Carbohydrates | 66g

Fat | 9g

> Melt coconut oil on medium heat in pan, add spices and sauté for 30 seconds. Stir in millet with spice mixture. Stir in almond milk and some water, bring to boil. Reduce heat to low, cover pan partially. Simmer for 15 minutes stirring often. Serve with honey on top.

Healthy Baked Oatmeal

Servings | 6

Per Serving

Calories | 285

Protein | 7g

Carbohydrates | 45g

Fat | 9g

2 ½ cups gluten-free rolled oats

1 ½ teaspoon baking powder

1 ½ teaspoon ground cinnamon

¼ cup honey

2 ½ cups unsweetened almond milk

2 teaspoon vanilla extract

2 ½ cups peeled and shredded carrots

1 ½ teaspoon grated fresh ginger

½ cup chopped walnuts

¼ cup raisins

Pinch of salt

> Preheat oven 375 degrees. Grease 11 x 8 dish. Combine together baking powder, oats, cinnamon and salt. In a different bowl, add in almond milk, honey and vanilla extract. Add almond mixture into oats mix, and mix very well.

> Mix in the carrots and ginger. Move the mixture into the dish and top it with raisins and walnuts evenly. Bake for approximately 35 minutes

Sweet Pineapple Muffins

Servings | 8

Per Serving

Calories | 235

Protein | 7g

Carbohydrates | 17g

Fat | 17g

2 cups almond flour

½ teaspoon baking soda

1 teaspoon ground cinnamon

3 eggs

2 tablespoons melted coconut oil

¼ cup honey

1 tablespoons fresh lemon juice

1 teaspoon vanilla extract

2/3 cup of fresh pineapple, chopped

1 large carrot, peeled and grated

> Preheat your oven to 325 degrees. Grease 8 cups of a muffin tin. In a bowl combine baking soda, flours, salt, and cinnamon.

> In a different bowl add in honey, eggs, coconut oil, lemon juice, vanilla extract and mix until very well combined.

> Add the egg mix in the flour mix and combine until very well mixed. Put in carrot and pineapple.

> Put the mixture into the muffin spaces evenly and bake for approximately 25 minutes.

Servings | 2

Per Serving

Calories | 215

Protein | 13g

Carbohydrates | 3g

Fat | 7g

Colorful Omelet

4 large eggs

1/8 teaspoon cayenne pepper

1 tablespoon olive oil

¼ teaspoon brown mustard seeds

1/8 teaspoon ground turmeric

2 chopped scallions

¼ cup plum tomato, chopped

Pinch of salt and pepper

> Combine the eggs and salt inside a bowl and mix very well, leave aside. Heat the olive oil in a cast iron skillet on medium heat. Add in the mustard seeds and turmeric, sauté approximately 30 seconds. Add in the plum tomato and cook for about 1 minute.

> Pour in the egg mixture evenly and cook for around 2 minutes. Tilt the pan to cook for an additional two minutes.

> Put the omelet on a place and cut into 2 pieces. Serve with salt and pepper on top.

Apple Salad Breakfast

Servings | 4

Per Serving

Calories | 202

Protein | 5g

Carbohydrates | 38g

Fat | 4g

4 tart green apples, cored and chopped

¼ cup slivered almonds, toasted

¼ cup dried cranberries

¼ cup dried cherries, chopped

1 (8 ounce) container vanilla yogurt

> Stir all the ingredients together in a bowl until evenly coated.

LUNCH RECIPES

Super Food Salad

Servings | 4

Per Serving

Calories | 320

Protein | 10g

Carbohydrates |59g

Fat | 10g

For the salad:

2 cups water

1 cup wheat berries

1 cup mango, peeled, cubed

1 cup pineapple, chopped

1 red bell pepper, seeded and chopped

½ cup mint leaves, chopped

½ cup cranberries

½ cup walnuts, toasted and chopped

For the dressing:

1 tablespoon ginger, minced

½ cup plain Green yogurt, 2%

3 tablespoons honey

½ teaspoon apple cider vinegar

Salt and pepper to taste

> For the salad in a pan, put the berries and water in and bring to boil. Cover it and cook for around 30 minutes. Remove and put aside to fully cool down. In a big bowl add wheat berries and remaining salad ingredients and mix. In a smaller bowl add dressing ingredients and combine well. Pour dressing over fruit mixture and toss well.

Creamy Spinach Soup

Servings | 6

Per Serving

Calories | 90

Protein | 6g

Carbohydrates | 81g

Fat | 4g

4 cups chicken broth

10 ounce frozen spinach

10 ounce frozen onion

6 celery stalks, chopped

½ teaspoon cayenne pepper

1/3 cup coconut cream

Salt and pepper

> In a big soup pan add all the broth and bring to boil on medium heat. Mix in the vegetables and again bring to boil.

> Slightly reduce heat and cook for about 5 minutes, stirring often. Reduce heat to low and simmer for 12 minutes. Stir and

> mix in coconut cream and immediately remove from heat, serve immediately.

Savory Beets Soup

Servings | 4

Per Serving

Calories | 100

Protein | 6g

Carbohydrates | 18g

Fat | 1g

¾ pound medium sized beets

2 small cucumbers, peeled and chopped

½ cup dill

2 tablespoons red onion

2 garlic cloves, chopped

2 tablespoons apple cider vinegar

2 cups vegetable broth

Salt and pepper

> In pan of water add beets on high heat and bring to boil. Reduce heat to low and simmer to 1 hour. Drain very well and keep beets aside to fully cool.

> Remove the skin of the beets, using a blender add beet and remaining ingredients until fully smooth. Serve.

Tempting Zucchini

Servings | 4

Per Serving

Calories | 85

Protein | 2g

Carbohydrates | 5g

Fat | 7g

2 garlic cloves, minced

1 small jalapeño pepper, seeded and minced

¼ cup vegetable broth

2 table spoons olive oil

½ teaspoon ground cumin

¼ teaspoon paprika

1 pound crosswise zucchini, sliced

1 tablespoon lemon juice

> Preheat your oven to 350 degrees. In a big bowl combine all ingredients except for zucchini and lemon juice

> Add zucchini slices and coat with garlic mix. Place zucchini slices in a baking dish, pour remaining mixture over zucchini evenly.

> Cover the baking dish and cook for about 5 minutes. Coat the zucchini slices with the mixture fully and bake uncovered for 5-10 more minutes.

> Serve hot with lemon juice drizzled over top.

Sautéed Asparagus

Servings | 4

Per Serving

Calories | 60

Protein | 3g

Carbohydrates | 6g

Fat | 3g

1 tablespoon coconut oil

2 garlic cloves

1 teaspoon cumin seeds

1 pound asparagus, trimmed and cut into 2-inch pieces

1 tablespoon ginger

2 teaspoon lemon juice

¼ teaspoon cayenne pepper

Salt and pepper

> Melt coconut oil on medium heat in a skillet. Add cumin seeds and garlic and sauté for 60 seconds.

> Add remaining ingredients and stir for about 10 minutes. Serve Immediately.

Kale Salad

Servings | 4

Per Serving

Calories | 150

Protein | 5g

Carbohydrates | 13g

Fat | 10g

6 cups kale, chopped

½ lemon

1 tablespoon olive oil

2 tablespoons red onion, minced

2 tablespoons green onion, minced

1 cucumber, thinly sliced

1 garlic clove, minced

¼ cup kalamata olives, chopped

> Cut the kale into small strips. Lightly steam the kale for 5-7 minutes in a steamer basket. Transfer to different bowl then add in basil, salt, lemon, oil, and toss it.

> Add in all the remaining ingredients. Mix well and serve.

Herbed Chicken

Servings | 4

Per serving

Calories | 300

Protein | 33g

Carbohydrates | 6g

Fat | 15g

2 tablespoons coconut oil

2 shallots, chopped

4 garlic cloves, minced,

½ teaspoon ginger

1 pound grass-fed chicken

2 jalapeño peppers, chopped and seeded

1 teaspoon honey

½ cup basil, chopped

1 tablespoon lime juice

Salt and pepper

> Melt the coconut oil on medium heat in a skillet. Add the shallots and sauté for a couple minutes. Add the ginger and garlic and sauté for 60 seconds.

> Add the chicken and cook for 5-8 minutes. Stir in the jalapeño peppers and honey and cook for 5 minutes, stirring often.

> Mix in the remaining ingredients and stir well, serve hot.

10 Smoothie Recipes

Directions for all smoothies:

Blend in blender until fully smooth.

Papaya Pineapple Blast

Servings | 1

Per Serving

Calories | 490

Protein | 15g

Carbohydrates | 53g

Fat | 28g

1 cup mixed greens

½ cup papayas

½ cup pineapple

3 strawberries

½ teaspoon coconut oil

1 handful cashews

1 ½ cups coconut water

Green Super Smoothie

Servings | 1

Per serving

Calories | 240

Protein| 8g

Carbohydrates| 37g

Fat | 9g

1 handful of spinach

½ a lime

1 stalk of celery

1 cup cucumber, chopped

½ cup pineapple, chopped

2 tablespoons flax seeds

3 ice cubes

1 ½ cups coconut water

Berry Beat Blast

Servings | 1

Per serving

Calories | 230

Protein |3g

Carbohydrates | 9g

Fat | 21g

2/3 cup beats

1 cup strawberries

1 teaspoon turmeric

½ teaspoon ginger

2 cups coconut water

1 orange

Hearty Green

Servings | 1

Per Serving

Calories | 240

Protein | 7g

Carbohydrates |32g

Fat | 11g

1 cup spinach

1 dash wheatgrass

3 chunks of pineapple

½ banana

1 tablespoon walnuts

1 teaspoon chia seeds

5 cherries

1 ½ cups green tea, cooled

Anti-Inflammation Blend

Servings | 1

Per Serving

Calories | 425

Protein | 20g

Carbohydrates | 45g

Fat | 21g

1 cup swiss chard

½ cup frozen pineapple

½ cup frozen cherries

2 tablespoons walnuts

¼ inch turmeric

2 teaspoons cocoa powder

2 tablespoons SuperFood protein blend+

1 cup coconut water

½ cup water

Energizer Smoothie

Servings | 1

Per Serving

Calories | 465

Protein | 10g

Carbohydrates | 56g

Fat | 25g

2 handfuls kale

½ avocado

¼ cup oats

1 tablespoon flax seeds

1 apple

1/3 cup blueberries

1 ½ cups unsweetened almond milk

Turmerific   Immune Boost

Servings | 1	Servings | 1
Per Serving	**Per serving**
Calories | 230	Calories | 160
Protein | 5g	Protein | 5g
Carbohydrates | 48g	Carbohydrates | 28g
Fat |5g	Fat | 5g

1 cup spinach	½ cup blueberries
1 chunk pineapple	1 cup spinach
1 chunk papayas	½ cup papayas
¼ lime	1 tablespoon chia seeds
¼ grapefruit	½ teaspoon ginger
¼ lemon	½ teaspoon turmeric
1 tablespoon flax seeds	¼ teaspoon cayenne pepper
½ teaspoon turmeric	1 ½ cups green tea
1 ½ cups water	

Flavonoid-Rich Mix

Servings | 1

Per Serving

Calories | 248

Protein | 6g

Carbohydrates | 30g

Fat | 14g

2 handfuls kale

½ cup blueberries

½ cup cherries

1 tablespoon flax seeds

3 walnuts

½ teaspoon turmeric

1 ½ cups water

Anti-Toxin Smoothie

Servings | 1

Per Serving

Calories | 380

Protein | 10g

Carbohydrates | 45g

Fat | 20g

½ cup frozen blueberries

1 cup kale

½ cup frozen cherries

1 tablespoon flax seeds

10 walnut halves

½ inch turmeric

1 ½ cups coconut water

Chicken Kebobs

Servings | 4

Per Serving

Calories | 180

Protein | 11g

Carbohydrates | 23g

Fat | 6g

1 pound boneless chicken breast, cubed

2 garlic cloves, minced

1 teaspoon paprika

1 teaspoon cayenne pepper

1 teaspoon ground cumin

½ teaspoon coriander

1 tablespoon olive oil

2 teaspoon balsamic vinegar

12 halved cherry tomatoes

Red bell pepper, seeded and cut into 1-inch pieces

Green bell pepper, seeded and cut into 1-inch pieces

Red onion, cut into 1-inch pieces

> In a big bowl mix together, ginger, garlic, spices, vinegar and oil to marinate chicken. Add the cubed chicken and marinate it well. Cover up and refrigerate for 60 minutes.

> Preheat your oven to 425 degrees and grease a large baking sheet. Remove the chicken from marinade. Add in the vegetables with the marinade and toss well.

> Thread vegetables and chicken onto presoaked 8 skewers. Put the skewers on the baking sheet and cook for about 10 minutes.

Gourmet Stuffed Bell Peppers

Servings | 4

Per Serving

Calories | 694

Protein | 31g

Carbohydrates | 130g

Fat | 7g

1 ½ cups cooked brown rice

1 (15-ounce) can of kidney beans, rinsed

4 medium bell peppers, tops and seeds removed

1 tablespoon coconut oil

2 teaspoons ground cumin

1 teaspoon ground turmeric

1 teaspoon garlic powder

1 teaspoon red chili powder

2 tablespoons parsley, chopped

Salt and pepper

> Preheat oven to 375 degrees and grease a large baking sheet. Melt the coconut oil in a large skillet on medium heat. Add the beans, cooked rice, and spices and cook for a few minutes. Stir in the parsley and remove from heat.

> Stuff each bell pepper with the rice mix evenly. Arrange the bell peppers on the baking sheet evenly.

> Bake for 20 minutes. Serve immediately

Savory Meatballs with Salad

Servings | 8

Per Serving

Calories | 164

Protein | 12g

Carbohydrates | 2g

Fat | 12g

For Meatballs:

1 pound lean turkey

1 tablespoon olive oil

1 teaspoon garlic, minced

2 tablespoons parsley, chopped

½ teaspoon cumin

1/2 teaspoon cayenne pepper

Pinch of salt

For Salad:

10 ounce mixed salad greens

2 tablespoons scallion, chopped

2 tablespoons mint, chopped

2 tablespoons oregano, chopped

2 tablespoons parsley, chopped

1 teaspoon mustard

¼ cup olive oil

> Preheat oven 400 degrees, put parchment paper on a large baking sheet. For the meatballs in a big bowl, add all the ingredients and mix very well.

> From the mixture, create 24 evenly sized meatballs and arrange them on the baking sheet.

> Bake around 15-20 minutes or until fully cooked.

> For the salad, combine all the ingredients together in a big bowl and toss well. Each serving will be 4 meat balls and some salad.

Chicken Soup

2 tablespoons olive oil

1 large onion, chopped

1 tablespoon ginger, minced

2 teaspoons cumin

1 teaspoon ground turmeric

Servings | 10

4 parsnips, peeled and chopped

Per Serving

2 large potatoes, peeled and chopped

Calories | 206

2 chopped zucchinis

Protein | 15g

1 cup shelled fresh peas

Carbohydrates | 22g

3 (4-ounce) skinless, boneless chicken breasts

Fat | 6g

5 cups chicken broth

5 cups water

½ cup cilantro, chopped

Salt and pepper, to taste

> Heat the oil on medium heat in a large soup pan. Add onion and sauté for 5 minutes. Add ginger and spices and sauté for 60 seconds. Stir in veggies and cook for 5 minutes. Add the water and broth and bring to boil.

> Reduce heat to low and simmer for 20 minutes. Using a slotted spoon put the chicken breasts in a bowl. Shred the chicken using 2 forks and put it in the simmering soup. Simmer for 10 minutes then stir in salt and pepper. Finished off by adding cilantro, serve hot.

Omega-3 Rich Burgers

For patties:

2 (5-ounce) finely chopped cooked salmon fillets

2 chopped scallions

2 minced garlic cloves

2 tablespoons chopped fresh dill

½ teaspoon of finely grated fresh lemon zest

2 organic eggs

2 tablespoons of fresh lemon juice

3 tablespoons of almond flour

2 teaspoons of Dijon mustard

1/8 teaspoons of cayenne pepper

Salt and freshly ground black pepper, to taste

1 tablespoon of olive oil

For Avocado Sauce:

1 peeled, pitted and chopped medium avocado

2 chopped garlic cloves

1 tbsp. of fresh dill

1 tsp. of Dijon mustard

1/8 tsp. of cayenne pepper

Salt and freshly ground black pepper, to taste

1 tbsp. of fresh lemon juice

3 tbsp. of olive oil

> For the burgers, add all the ingredients together in a bowl except for the oil and mix very well. Create 8 equal patties from the mixture. Heat the oil on high heat on a large skillet. Add the salmon patties on the skillet and cook for 5-8 minutes on each side.

> For the sauce add all the ingredients to a food processor except the oil and mix very well. While the motor is running pour in some water until the mixture becomes smooth. 2 burgers with sauce per serving.

Servings | 4

Per Serving

Calories | 392

Protein | 20g

Carbohydrates | 8g

Fat | 33g

Easy Baked Chicken Tenders

Servings | 4-6

Per Serving

Calories | 731

Protein | 41g

Carbohydrates | 36g

Fat | 47g

2 pounds chicken tenderloins

1 cup blanched almond flour

1 tablespoon flax meal

1 teaspoon paprika

½ teaspoon garlic powder

½ teaspoon sea salt

½ teaspoon parsley, dried

¼ teaspoon poultry seasoning

2 eggs

Olive oil, in a sprayer

Salt and pepper

> Pre-heat your oven to 425 degrees and put parchment paper on 2 large baking sheets. In a wide bowl mix the flax meal, almond flour, paprika, garlic powder, sea salt, poultry seasoning, parsley, and salt and pepper.

> In a different smaller bowl whip the 2 eggs. Using paper towels take the excess moisture from the chicken tenders and then dip them in the eggs. Coat the chicken tenders in the almond flour breading very well.

> Lightly spray the breaded chicken tenders with olive oil and evenly put them on the baking sheet. Bake for 10 minutes on each side, serve immediately.

Easy Scallops & Zucchini

2 tablespoons olive oil

2 garlic cloves, minced

3 zucchinis, cut into 2-inch pieces

1 ½ pounds baby scallops

1 large chopped tomato

2 sliced scallions

2 tablespoons of fresh lemon juice

Salt & pepper

> Heat the olive oil on high heat in a large skillet. Add rosemary and garlic and sauté for around 60 seconds. Add in the zucchini and cook for around 3 minutes.

> Using a slotted spoon transfer the zucchini into a bowl. Reduce the heat to medium and immediately add the scallops. Cook for 4 minutes, stirring often. Add tomato, zucchini and scallion and cook for 3 minutes. Drizzle lemon juice over top and serve.

Servings | 4

Per Serving

Calories | 248

Protein | 31g

Carbohydrates | 12g

Fat | 8g

2 tablespoons olive oil

2 large chicken breasts, diced into 1" cubes

1 bell pepper, any color

1 large white onion, diced

1 zucchini, diced into small chunks

1 tablespoon coconut aminos

1 teaspoon sriracha sauce

Handful pea shoots

Chicken Stir Fry

Servings | 3

Per Serving

Calories | 245

Protein | 35g

Carbohydrates |8g

Fat | 15g

> Heat the oil in a large cast iron pan. Once you add in the chicken cook it on medium heat for about 5 minutes. Add in peppers and onions for another 5 minutes. Add in zucchini and cook for another 5-7 minutes.

> Put in coconut aminos and mix well. Add sriracha sauce as well. Add in pea shoots and start tossing the mixture and cook for about 2-3 minutes. Serve immediately.

Chicken Tacos with Avocado Salsa

1 cup frozen corn, thawed

1 cup cherry tomatoes, quartered

2 teaspoon lime juice

8 taco shells, warmed

1 pound boneless, skinless chicken breast cut in ½ inch strips

1/3 cup water

1 teaspoon sugar

1 teaspoon chili powder

1 teaspoon onion powder

1 teaspoon oregano, dried

1 teaspoon ground cumin

1 teaspoon paprika

½ teaspoon salt

½ teaspoon garlic powder

1 ripe avocado, peeled and cubed

Servings | 4

Per Serving

Calories | 354

Protein | 37g

Carbohydrates | 30g

Fat | 15g

> Use cooking pray to coat a large skillet over medium-high heat. Brown chicken. Add sugar water and seasonings. Cook for 5 minutes stirring often, or until chicken is no longer pink.

> Mix the avocado, tomatoes, corn and lime juice in a bowl, spoon the chicken mixture into the taco shells, and top with avocado salsa.

BBQ Tuna Fritters

Servings | 2

Per serving

Calories | 371

Protein | 23g

Carbohydrates | 27g

Fat | 18g

1 (5 ounce) can light tuna in water, drained

1 egg

2/3 cup quick cooking oats

3 tablespoons bbq sauce

3 tablespoons green onion, chopped

½ teaspoon hot pepper sauce

½ teaspoon dried savory

1 pinch salt

2 tablespoons vegetable oil

> Stir together the tuna, oats and egg in a bowl until fully blended. Mix in green onion, bbq sauce, savory, hot pepper sauce and salt.

> In a large skillet heat the oil over medium heat. Spoon tablespoonfuls of the tuna mixture in the pan, slightly flatten. Smaller patties hold together better. Cook for 3 minutes on each side, or until browned. Serve.

Mandarin Chicken Pasta Salad

½ cucumber, halved lengthwise, seeded and sliced

½ cup diced red bell pepper

½ cup coarsely chopped red onion

2 diced Roma tomatoes

1 carrot, shredded

1 (6 ounce) bag spinach

1 (11 ounce) can mandarin orange segments, drained

2 cups cooked chicken, diced

½ cup sliced almonds, toasted

1 teaspoon ginger, chopped and peeled

1/3 cup rice vinegar

¼ cup orange juice

¼ cup vegetable oil

1 teaspoon toasted sesame oil

1 (1 ounce) package dry onion soup mix

2 teaspoons sugar

1 clove garlic, pressed

1 (8 ounce) package bow tie pasta

> To make the dressing, whisk together the vegetable oil, orange juice, rice vinegar, ginger root, soup mix, sesame oil, garlic and sugar until fully combined. Cover up and refrigerate until needed.

> Bring a large pot of lightly salted water to boil. Add bow tie pasta and cook for about 10 minutes. Drain, rinse under cold water, put pasta in large bowl. To make salad toss bell pepper, cucumber, tomatoes, onion, spinach, carrot, mandarin oranges, chicken and almonds with pasta. Pour dressing over top salad and toss to coat evenly, serve immediately.

Servings | 6

Per Serving

Calories | 425

Protein | 22g

Carbohydrates | 44g

Fat | 18g

Shrimp and Pineapple Ceviche

Servings | 4

Per Serving

Calories | 195

Protein | 15g

Carbohydrates | 17g

Fat | 8g

2 cups cooked shrimp, chopped

1 cup red bell pepper, chopped

1 cup pineapple, chopped

1 peeled avocado, pitted and chopped

½ red onion, chopped

½ bunch cilantro, chopped

1 garlic clove, minced

1 Serrano pepper, minced

2 limes, juiced

Salt and pepper to taste

> Stir the pineapple, bell pepper, shrimp, avocado, cilantro, onion, garlic, Serrano pepper, lime juice, salt and pepper in a ceramic mixing bowl until fully combined.

> Cover the bowl and refrigerate 1 hour before serving.

Green Bean and Potato Salad

Servings | 10

Per Serving

Calories | 176

Protein | 2g

Carbohydrates |17g

Fat | 11g

1 ½ pounds red potatoes

¾ pounds green beans, trimmed and snapped

¼ cup basil, chopped

1 small red onion, chopped

Salt and pepper

¼ cup balsamic vinegar

2 tablespoons Dijon Mustard

2 tablespoons lemon juice

1 clove garlic, minced

1 dash Worcestershire sauce

½ cup extra virgin olive oil

> Put the potatoes in a large pot and fill with 1 inch of water, bring to boil. Cook for 15 minutes or until tender. Add in green beans to steam after the first 10 minutes. Drain, cool and cut potatoes into quarters. Transfer to large bowl and toss with red onion, basil, salt and pepper, leave aside.

> Whisk together the balsamic vinegar, mustard, garlic, lemon juice, Worcestershire sauce, and olive oil. Pour over salad and stir to coat. Serve.

California Sandwich

4 slices whole wheat bread, lightly toasted

1 avocado, sliced

1 cup mushrooms, sliced

1/3 cup sliced toasted almonds

1 tomato, sliced

4 slices Swiss cheese

Servings | 4

Per Serving

Calories | 335

Protein | 15g

Carbohydrates | 21g

Fat | 22g

> Preheat your oven broiler. Put the toasted bread on a baking sheet. On top of each slice of bread put ¼ avocado, almonds, mushrooms, and tomato slices. Then top each with Swiss cheese.

> Broil the sandwiches until the cheese melts, should be 2 minutes. Serve immediately.

Shrimp Noodle Soup

2 teaspoons vegetable oil

1 onion, chopped

2 garlic cloves, minced

1 tablespoon ginger, minced

1 pinch red pepper, crushed

2 quarts chicken broth

1 cup sliced carrots

1 cup celery, sliced

2 cups snow peas

12 ounces shrimp, peeled and deveined

4 ounces rice Vermicelli

2 tablespoons soy sauce

¼ teaspoon black pepper

> Over medium heat in a saucepan cook ginger, garlic, onion and red pepper in oil for 2 minutes. Pour in broth, celery, carrots and bring to boil. Reduce the heat, cover, and simmer for 5 minutes.

> Stir in the shrimp and snow peas, cover and cook 3 minutes. Break noodles into 2-inch pieces and stir into soup, cover and cook 3 minutes more until vegetables are tender and shrimp is pink. Stir in pepper and soy sauce to serve.

Servings | 6

Per Serving

Calories | 139

Protein | 11g

Carbohydrates | 18g

Fat | 2g

Sweet Potato Fries

Servings | 4

Per Serving

Calories | 226

Protein | 4g

Carbohydrates | 45g

Fat | 3g

2 large sweet potatoes, peeled and cut into French-fry sized pieces

1 tablespoon olive oil

2 tablespoons rosemary, minced

Salt and pepper to taste

> Preheat oven to 425 degrees. Toss together in a bowl the sweet potatoes, olive oil, rosemary, salt and pepper and arrange on a baking sheet. Bake for 20-30 minutes or until tender.

Romaine Rice Tuna Salad

Servings | 4

Per serving

Calories | 522

Protein | 20g

Carbohydrates | 80g

Fat | 12g

2 cups long grain white rice

4 cups water

1 head romaine lettuce, chopped

1 large carrot, grated

1 (7 ounce) can albacore tuna in water, drained and flaked

3 tablespoons olive oil

4 tablespoons balsamic vinegar

¼ teaspoon salt

¼ teaspoon pepper

1 teaspoon chopped green onions

> Combine rice and water in a saucepan, bring to boil. Reduce the heat to low, cover, and simmer for 20 minutes, or till rice is tender and water is absorbed.

> Toss together in a bowl the carrot, romaine lettuce and tuna. Pour the olive oil and vinegar over this mixture, and also salt and pepper. Toss fully. When rice is finished, cool down for 5 minutes, and then toss with the salad. Serve immediately.

Millet-Stuffed Peppers

1 cup millet

4 cups water

5 medium bell peppers

3 medium tomatoes, chopped

4 cubes vegetable bouillon

1 (15 ounce) can black beans, drained

Servings | 5

Per Serving

Calories | 189

Protein | 6g

Carbohydrates | 37g

Fat | 2g

> In a saucepan combine the water, bouillons, and millet, bring to boil. Reduce heat to low, cover, and simmer for 15 minutes or until water is absorbed.

> Slice the tops off the peppers and remove the seeds and cores and set aside. When the millet is finished stir in the black beans and tomatoes. Spoon into the peppers until filled. Put the peppers onto a glass baking dish and cover with plastic wrap. Cook in the microwave for 10 minutes or until tender. Turn pepper every couple minutes to ensure cooking. Serve.

DINNER RECIPES

Fabulous Chicken & Sweet Potatoes

For Sweet Potatoes:

2 tablespoons lime juice

2 medium sweet potatoes, chopped

1 tsp lime zest, grated

2 garlic cloves, minced

2 tablespoons of olive oil

For Chicken Legs:

4 chicken legs

1 small onion, chopped

1 minced garlic clove

¼ tsp ginger, minced

¼ teaspoon ground cumin

2 tablespoons olive oil

2 tablespoons of fresh lemon juice

Salt and pepper

> Starting with the chicken, mix all the chicken ingredients in a bowl except for the chicken legs. Add the chicken and coat them fully. Refrigerate to marinade for 1-2 hours. Preheat your oven to 375 degrees and prepare a large baking dish.

> Take the chicken out of the fridge and let it sit for 30 minutes before baking. Arrange the chopped sweet potatoes around the chicken legs on the baking dish. For sweet potatoes in a different bowl add all ingredients and toss and coat fully. Cover the baking dish with foil and bake for 30 minutes. Remove foil and bake for additional 15 minutes.

Servings | 4

Per Serving

Calories | 547

Protein | 51g

Carbohydrates | 21g

Fat | 26g

Family Lentil Soup

4 cups spinach, chopped

1 tablespoon lemon juice

Salt and pepper

1 tablespoon olive oil

1 large onion, minced

5 minced garlic cloves

½ teaspoon ground turmeric

¼ teaspoon red pepper flakes, crushed

4 cups vegetable broth

1 cup red lentil

2 ½-inch sized sweet potatoes, peeled and cubed

> Heat the olive oil on medium heat in a large soup pan. Add garlic and onion and sauté for a few minutes. Stir in red pepper flakes and turmeric and sauté for 60 seconds. Add in the broth and lentil and bring to boil

> Reduce the heat to low and simmer for about 15 minutes, covered. Add in sweet potatoes and simmer for another 10 minutes. Stir in spinach and simmer for 3-5 minutes. Stir in salt and pepper and remove from heat, mixing in the lemon juice to finish

Servings | 4

Per Serving

Calories | 356

Protein | 19g

Carbohydrates | 56g

Fat | 5g

Savory Trout

Servings | 6

Per Serving

Calories | 480

Protein | 60g

Carbohydrates | 2g

Fat | 24g

2 (1 ½ pound) trout, gutted and cleaned

1 sliced lemon

2 tablespoons dill, minced

2 tablespoons olive oil

2 tablespoons lemon juice

Salt and pepper

> Preheat your oven to 425 degrees. Arrange the wire rack in a foil lined baking sheet. Sprinkle your trout with salt and pepper, both inside and out.

> Fill the fish cavity with dill and lemon slices. Put the trouth on the baking sheet and drizzle with lemon juice. Bake for 25-27 minutes.

Easy Scallops & Zucchini

2 tablespoons olive oil

2 garlic cloves, minced

3 zucchinis, cut into 2-inch pieces

1 ½ pounds baby scallops

1 large chopped tomato

2 sliced scallions

2 tablespoons of fresh lemon juice

Salt & pepper

> Heat the olive oil on high heat in a large skillet. Add rosemary and garlic and sauté for around 60 seconds. Add in the zucchini and cook for around 3 minutes.

> Using a slotted spoon transfer the zucchini into a bowl. Reduce the heat to medium and immediately add the scallops. Cook for 4 minutes, stirring often. Add tomato, zucchini and scallion and cook for 3 minutes. Drizzle lemon juice over top and serve.

Servings | 4

Per Serving

Calories | 248

Protein | 31g

Carbohydrates | 12g

Fat | 8g

Smoky Steak with Salsa

Servings | 4

Per Serving

Calories | 273

Protein | 32g

Carbohydrates | 4g

Fat | 13g

For Steak:

1 (1-pound) grass-fed flank steak, trimmed

2 garlic cloves, minced

½ teaspoon garlic powder

½ teaspoon ginger powder

½ teaspoon ground cumin

½ teaspoon ground coriander

¼ teaspoon cayenne pepper

2 tablespoons lemon juice

Salt and pepper

For Salsa:

¾ cup yellow grape tomatoes, quartered

¾ cup red grape tomatoes, quartered

¼ cup red onion, chopped

2 tablespoons cilantro, chopped

1 tablespoon lemon juice

1 tablespoon olive oil

Salt and pepper

> To start, mix together the lemon juices, spices, and garlic in a bowl. Coat the steak with the mixture fully. Set aside for 30 minutes.

> Preheat the grill to high heat and grease the grill grate. Cook the steak for about 6 minutes on each side. Remove from grill pan and set aside for 5 minutes before slicing.

> In the meantime mix all the salsa ingredients in a bowl.

> Cut the steak into desired slices. Top with salsa.

Nutritious Salmon Salad

Servings | 4

Per Serving

Calories | 271

Protein | 26g

Carbohydrates |13g

Fat | 13g

1 pound green been, trimmed

¼ cup red wine vinegar

2 tablespoons Dijon mustard

1 tablespoon olive oil

1 tablespoon shallots, minced

¼ teaspoon salt, divided

¼ teaspoon pepper, divided

4 (3-ounce) salmon fillets

4 cups mixed salad greens

¼ cup vertically sliced Vidalia

2 hard-cooked large eggs, sliced

> Preheat your grill to medium high heat. Put the beans on a large pan of boiling water and cook for 2 minutes. Drain and plunge the beans into ice water, then drain again.

> Combine the mustard, vinegar, oil, shallots, 1/8 teaspoon salt, 1/8 pepper in a bowl and stir fully, leave aside.

> Spray both sides of each fillet with olive oil using a mister and then sprinkle 1/8 of salt and pepper over top. Put the fish skin side up on the grill and cook fully for 8 minutes.

> Put 1cup of salad greens into 4 different bowls. Top with egg slices, beans, onion, and then top with the salmon. Drizzle with dressing to serve.

Veggie Stew with Dumplings

For Dumplings:

100g flour

50g unsalted butter

50g cheddar cheese, grated

2 teaspoons rosemary, chopped

1 teaspoon thyme leaves

1 tablespoon olive oil

350g shallot, peeled

2 leeks, thickly sliced

½ swede, chopped in chunks

2 parsnips, quartered

350g Chantenay carrot

175g pearl barley

225ml white wine

1 l vegetable stock

1 bay leaf

3 sprigs thyme

Small bunch parsley, chopped

> Heat the olive oil in a big casserole dish and add the shallots and cook for 5-7 minutes or until soft and brown. Add leeks for 2 minutes, and then add in carrots, swede and parsnips. Pour in the wine and barley and cook until wine has reduced to half. Add the bay, thyme, parsley, stock and seasoning and cover it to bring to boil.

> Simmer for 45-50 minutes or until veg and barley are tender. Stir often. Preheat oven to 200 degrees and prepare dumplings in meantime. Rub the butter and flour together to create breadcrumbs. Add in remaining ingredients and combine fully. Pour in 2 tablespoons water until you have a soft dough mix. Divide into six and roll into balls. Dot on top of stew and transfer to oven. Cook for 25 minutes or until dumplings are golden.

Servings | 6

Per Serving

Calories | 391

Protein | 10g

Carbohydrates | 57g

Fat | 14g

Turkey Pasta

Servings | 6

Per Serving

Calories | 652

Protein | 32g

Carbohydrates | 80g

Fat | 22g

¼ cup olive oil

350g shallot, peeled

1 onion, chopped

4 garlic cloves, minced

1 carrot, peeled and chopped

1 pound cooked turkey, shredded

3 cups marinara

¼ cup basil leaves, chopped

1 pound spaghetti

Grated parmesan cheese

Salt and pepper

> Heat olive oil over large frying pan on medium heat. Add the garlic and onion and sauté for about 5 minutes. Add the celery and carrot, sauté for 5 minutes. Add the turkey and sauté for 60 seconds. Add marinara sauce. Decrease heat to low and simmer for 15 minutes, stirring occasionally. Stir in the basil. Season with salt and pepper.

> In the meantime, cook the spaghetti in a big pot of boiling salted water until fully cooked, about 8 minutes. Add the pasta to the sauce and coat fully. Serve with parmesan.

Roasted Bell Pepper and Olive Pizza

Servings | 12

Per Serving

Calories | 104

Protein | 4g

Carbohydrates | 15g

Fat | 3g

2 (1-pound) Italian cheese-flavoured pizza crust

2 large red bell peppers

2 large yellow bell peppers

½ cup green olives, sliced

¼ cup parsley, chopped

2 teaspoons drained capers

2 teaspoons red wine vinegar

¾ teaspoon olive oil

1/8 teaspoon black pepper

6 tablespoons parmesan cheese

> Preheat your broiler and cut the bell peppers in half, vertically, take out the seeds and membranes. Place them skin sides up on a foil lined baking sheet, flatten with your hand. Broil for 15 minutes or until blackened. Put them in a zip top bag, sealing, and let it sit aside for 15 minutes. Cut and peel the peppers into strips and put them in a bowl. Add in the green olives, parsley, capers, vinegar, olive oil and black pepper and combine well.

> Preheat your oven to 350 degrees. Spread the bell pepper mix evenly on pizza crusts. Sprinkle with cheese. Bake for 7-8 minutes or until the cheese melts. Cut into 12 pieces.

Yummy Lasagna

1 pound turkey sausage

¾ pound lean ground turkey

½ cup onion, minced

2 garlic cloves, crushed

1 (28-ounce) can crushed tomatoes

2 (6-ounce) cans tomato paste

2 (6.5-ounce) cans canned tomato sauce

½ cup water

1 ½ teaspoons dried basil leaves

½ teaspoon fennel seeds

1 teaspoon Italian seasoning

¼ teaspoon black pepper

2 tablespoons parsley, chopped

12 lasagna noodles

16 ounces ricotta cheese

¾ pound low-fat mozzarella cheese, sliced

¾ cup parmesan cheese, grated

> Heat a skillet over medium heat, and cook the turkey sausage, ground turkey, onion, garlic, stirring for 15 minutes. Stir in tomato paste, water, tomato sauce, crushed tomatoes. Season with fennel seeds, basil, Italian seasoning, 2 tablespoons parsley, pepper. Simmer for 1 ½ hours, uncovered, stirring occasionally.

> Preheat your oven to 350 degrees. Boil a large pot of water using a bit of salt. Cook the lasagna until fully cooked, 8 minutes approximately. Drain.

> Spread 1 ½ cups turkey sauce in the bottom of a 9x13 baking dish. Arrange 6 noodles vertically over the sauce. Spread half the ricotta over the noodles. Put 1/3 of the mozzarella cheese slices over top. With a spoon put 1 ½ cups turkey sauce over mozzarella and sprinkle ¼ cup parmesan. Repeat layers and top with remaining parmesan and mozzarella cheese.

> Bake in oven until cheese melts, about 25 minutes. Remove foil and bake addition 25 minutes. Let it cool before serving.

Servings | 12

Per Serving

Calories | 390

Protein | 33g

Carbohydrates | 33g

Fat | 15g

Spicy Chicken Chili

4 cups chicken broth, divided

2 (15-ounce) cans black beans, rinsed and drained

1 tablespoon olive oil

1 large onion, chopped

2 medium poblano peppers, seeded and chopped

Servings | 6

Per Serving

1 jalapeño pepper, seeded and chopped

4 garlic cloves, minced

Calories | 696

1 tablespoon ground cumin

Protein | 61g

½ tablespoon ancho chili powder

Carbohydrates |94g

1 ½ teaspoon coriander

Fat | 8g

4 cups shredded, cooked chicken

1 tablespoon lime juice

¼ cup cilantro, chopped

> Add 1 cup of broth and 1 can of black beans in food processor and pulse fully. Put in a bowl and leave aside. Heal the oil on medium heat in a large pan. Add in poblano, onion, jalapeño and sauté for 5 minutes. Add spices garlic and a bit of salt and sauté for 1 minute.

> Add the beans mix and remaining broth and bring to boil. Reduce heat to low and simmer for 20 minutes. Stir in chicken, lime juice, remaining can of beans and bring to boil. Reduce heat to low, simmer for 8 minutes. Serve with cilantro to top.

Burgers with Mushrooms and Radicchio

1 tablespoon olive oil

1 pound mixed exotic mushrooms, trimmed

¼ teaspoon salt

¾ teaspoon black pepper, divided

1 ¼ pounds sirloin

¼ teaspoon salt, divided

4 (2ounce) whole-wheat hamburger buns

1 small head radicchio, sliced in thin rings

Servings | 4

Per Serving

Calories | 473

Protein | 38g

Carbohydrates |38g

Fat | 20g

> Heat oil over medium heat in a large skillet. Add ¼ teaspoon each of salt and pepper and the mushrooms and cook for 5 minutes, stirring often. Put the mushrooms on a plate and wipe out skillet, reserve.

> Create 4 meat patties with your hand and sprinkle remaining ½ teaspoon pepper over both sides of burger. Put the skillet to high heat and cook burgers for 5-7 minutes. Put ¼ off the radicchio slices, then the burgers, on bottom side buns. Divide mushrooms evenly among burgers and other top of bun.

Healthy Chicken Burritos

Servings | 4

Per Serving

Calories | 315

Protein | 17g

Carbohydrates | 15g

Fat | 21g

2 cups cooked chicken, shredded

½ cup Mexican cheese blend (or mozzarella)

1 avocado, diced

2 tablespoons cilantro, chopped

4 large tortillas

1 tablespoons oil

> Mix the cheese, cilantro, shredded chicken, and avocados. Lay a flat tortilla on a plate and add ¼ the mixture, do this 4 times for 4 tortillas.

> Pour 1 tablespoon of the oil in a heated pan. Put all the tortilla roles on the pan and cook on high heat for about 2 minutes, flip over and cook opposite sides for another 2 minutes or until golden. Serve hot.

Lemon Asparagus Risotto

1 stalk celery, diced

2 tablespoons lemon juice

¼ teaspoon salt, ¼ teaspoon pepper

½ teaspoon lemon zest

20 asparagus spear, trimmed

1 garlic clove, minced

4 cups sodium-reduced chicken broth

1 cup Arborio rice

2 tablespoons olive oil

1 small onion, diced

½ cup dry white wine

¼ cup parmesan cheese, grated

Servings | 4

Per Serving

Calories | 357

Protein | 11g

Carbohydrates | 53g

Fat | 8g

> Put a steamer into a saucepan and fill with water to below the bottom of the steamer. Bring water to boil. Add the asparagus and cover. Steam for about 5 minutes, or tender. Cut the asparagus into 1-inch piece and leave aside.

> Heat the chicken broth over medium heat in a saucepan and keep at a simmer whilst preparing the risotto. Heat the olive oil over medium heat in a large skillet. Cook and stir celery and onion for about 5 minutes, or until tender. Season with the salt and pepper. Stir in Arborio rice and garlic. Cook additional 5 minutes, or till rice is slightly toasted.

> Pour the white wine into the rice mix, stirring often until liquid evaporates, around 5 minutes. Stir the chicken broth into the rice, stirring often for 20 minutes. Add asparagus and stir. Once you remove from heat top with lemon zest, parmesan cheese and lemon juice.

Baked Parmesan Fish

Servings | 4

Per Serving

Calories | 192

Protein | 31g

Carbohydrates | 4g

Fat | 5g

16 ounces fish fillets

1 egg

2 tablespoons milk

For Breading:

1/3 cup parmesan cheese, grated

2 tablespoons flour

½ teaspoon paprika

¼ teaspoon salt

1/8 teaspoon pepper

> Beat the milk and egg inside a bowl and set aside. Combine all the breading ingredients in a zipper bag. Dip fillets in egg one at a time and shake in breading in bag.

> Bake uncovered on an oiled baking sheet for 25 minutes at 350 degrees. Serve hot.

Broccoli and Garlic Pasta

Servings | 4

Per Serving

Calories | 226

Protein | 7g

Carbohydrates | 47g

Fat | 2g

1 cup chicken broth

½ teaspoon dried basil

2 garlic cloves minced

3 cups broccoli florets

4 ½ cups hot cooked penne

1 tablespoon lemon juice

A bit of parmesan cheese and black pepper

> Combine Broth, pepper, basil, broccoli and garlic in a large skillet, bring to boil. Cover and cook for 3 minutes on low heat or until broccoli is tender.

> Add lemon juice and hot cooked pasta, toss to coat and serve with parmesan.

Crunchy Chickpeas

Servings | 8

Per Serving

Calories | 95

Protein | 3g

Carbohydrates | 11g

Fat | 4g

2 (15 ½ - ounce) cans chickpeas, rinsed and drained

2 tablespoons canola oil

1 teaspoon ground turmeric

¾ teaspoon salt

¼ teaspoon ground red pepper

1/8 teaspoon onion powder

1 garlic clove, minced

> Preheat your oven to 300 degrees. Wrap the chickpeas in a towel and lightly roll to loosen skins. Discard skins.

> Mix chickpeas and remaining ingredients. Arrange on baking sheet. Bake for 1 hour and 40 minutes, stirring every 20-30 minutes.

Apple Cinnamon Pork Chops

Servings | 4

Per Serving

Calories | 316

Protein | 22g

Carbohydrates |31g

Fat | 12g

2 tablespoons reduced-fat butter, divided

4 (4-ounce) boneless pork loin chops

3 tablespoons brown sugar

1 teaspoon cinnamon

½ teaspoon ground nutmeg

¼ teaspoon salt

4 medium tart apples, thinly sliced

2 tablespoons pecans, chopped

> Heat 1 Tbsp butter on medium heat in a large skillet. Add porkchops, cook 5 minutes on each side. Mix cinnamon, brown sugar, nutmeg and salt in a bowl. Remove chops, keep warm. Add pecans, apples, brown sugar mixture and remaining butter to pan. Cook until apple are tender, serve with pork chops

Pork Chops with Honey-Garlic Sauce

Servings | 4

Per Serving

Calories |249

Protein | 27g

Carbohydrates |19g

Fat | 7g

4 (6-ounce) bone-in pork loin chops

¼ cup lemon juice

¼ cup honey

2 tablespoons reduced-sodium soy sauce

1 garlic clove, minced

> Cook pork chops on medium heat in a large skillet, 6 minutes on each side. Remove and let them sit for a few minutes. Combine remaining ingredients and add to pan. Cook for 4 minutes, stirring often, serve with chops.

Chicken and Sprouts Stir fry

¾ cup carrot, chopped

3 tablespoons reduced-sodium soy sauce

3 tablespoons honey

1 ¼ lbs. Boneless, skinless, chicken breasts

2 cups beans sprouts, rinsed and dried

2 ½ tablespoons vegetable oil, divided

1 ½ teaspoons gingerroot, minced and pared

2 garlic cloves, minced

¾ cup scallion, chopped

Servings | 4

Per Serving

Calories | 325

Protein | 33g

Carbohydrates | 21g

Fat | 12g

> In a large frying pan heat 1 ½ tablespoons of oil on high heat. Add the sprouts and cook stirring often until tender, about 1-2 minutes. Put the sprouts on a plate and keep warm.

> In the same pan add remaining oil and for 30-60 seconds. Add the garlic, carrots, chicken and ginger and stir fry for 2 minutes. Add the scallions and continue frying until the chicken is tender on all sides, about 2-3 minutes. Add honey and soy sauce and mix well, cook, stirring often for 1 more minute. Top warm sprouts with chicken mixture

Creamy Ham Penne

Servings | 4

Per Serving

Calories | 371

Protein | 25g

Carbohydrates | 49g

Fat | 8g

2 cups whole wheat penne pasta, uncooked

2 broccoli florets

1 cup fat-free milk

1 package (6 ½ ounces) reduced-fat, garlic-herb, spreadable cheese

1 cup fully cooked ham, cubed

¼ teaspoon pepper

> Cook the penne according to its package instructions in a large pan, adding in the florets during the last 5 minutes of cooking. Drain, remove and leave aside. In same pan combine the cheese and milk, cooking stirring often, over medium heat for 4-5 minutes or until cheese melts fully. Add the ham, penne, and pepper mixture heat through.

Baked Potato & Broccoli Soup

Servings | 7

Per serving

Calories | 223

Protein | 17g

Carbohydrates | 20g

Fat | 7g

¼ cup all-purpose flour

2 (14-¼ ounce) low-sodium, fat-free chicken broth

3 cups peeled, cubed potato (1 ¼ lbs.)

2 cups broccoli florets, chopped

1 small onion, chopped

1 ¼ cups reduced-fat milk

1 (8-ounce) block, reduced fat cheddar cheese, shredded

1 teaspoon reduced fat cheddar cheese

1 teaspoon fully cooked bacon pieces

1 teaspoon chopped green onions

> Whisk 1/3 chicken broth and the flour until fully smooth. Combine remaining chicken broth and next 3 ingredients in a Dutch oven. Bring to boil. Cover and reduce heat and simmer 8 minutes or till potatoes are tender. Slowly mix in the flour mixture and cook for 5 minutes stirring often.

> Stir in 8 ounces of cheese and milk, cook mixture over medium heat, stirring often, until cheese melts fully. Top each serving of soup with 1 tsp cheese, 1 tsp bacon, 1 tsp onions

Spaghetti and Meatballs

For Sauce:

Cooking spray

1 cup onion, chopped

3 minced garlic clove

2 tablespoons tomato paste

¼ teaspoon salt

1 (14-ounce) can sodium-reduced beef broth

2 (28-ounce) cans whole peeled tomatoes, undrained and chopped

Servings | 8

Per Serving

Calories | 291

Protein | 24g

Carbohydrates | 32g

Fat | 8g

For Meatballs:

1 (1-ounce) slice white bread

2 (4-ounce) links sweet turkey Italian sausage, casings removed

½ cup chopped onion

1/3 cup basil, chopped

¼ cup parsley, chopped

2 tablespoons egg substitute

½ teaspoon ground black pepper, ¼ tsp salt

2 garlic cloves, minced

1 large egg

1 pound ground sirloin

Remaining Ingredients:

½ chopped parsley

1/3 cup chopped basil

1 pound hot cooked spaghetti

½ cup (2 ounces) grated Parmigiano,-Regganio

> Prepare sauce by heating large skillet over medium heat and coat with cooking spray. Add 1 cup onion and sauté for 3 minutes. Add 3 garlic cloves, sauté for 60 seconds. Add tomato paste cook for 1 minute. Stir in ¼ tsp salt and broth, cook 4 minutes. Stir in tomatoes, reduce heat and simmer 45 minutes, stirring often. Preheat broiler.

> Prepare meatballs, put bread in food processor, process till bread crumbs measure ½ cup. Combine crumbs, sausage, ½ cup onion, and next 8 ingredients (through sirloin) in a bowl. Shape sirloin mixture into 32 meatballs. Put on broiler pan, broil for 15 mins. or until done. Add meatballs to sauce, simmer 15 minutes. Top with ½ cup parsley, 1/3 cup basil, serve over spaghetti, sprinkle cheese over.

SNACK
RECIPES

Baked Tortilla Chips

Servings | 6

Per Serving

Calories | 147

Protein | 3g

Carbohydrates |26g

Fat | 4g

1 (12-ounce) package corn tortillas

1 tablespoon vegetable oil

3 tablespoons lime juice

1 teaspoon ground cumin

1 teaspoon chili powder

1 teaspoon salt

> Preheat oven to 350 degrees. Cut each tortilla in 8 chip sized wedges on a cookie sheet. In a mister combine the lime juice and oil, Mix and spray each tortilla wedge till lightly moist.

> Combine cumin, chili powder, salt in a bowl and sprinkle on tortillas. Bake for around 7 minutes. Rotate pan and bake additional 8 minutes. Serve.

Peanut Butter Nuggets

Servings | 30

Per Serving

Calories |46

Protein | 2g

Carbohydrates |3g

Fat | 2g

½ cup natural peanut butter

¼ cup non-fat dry milk powder

¼ cup unsweetened flaked coconut

1/3 cup rolled oats

½ teaspoon ground cinnamon

¼ cup unsweetened apple juice concentrate, thawed

> Combine milk powder, peanut butter, and coconut in large bowl. Stir in cinnamon, oats, wheat germ and juice concentrate until fully combined. Shape mixture into 1-inch balls. Chill fully before serving, store leftovers in fridge.

Servings | 60

Per Serving

Calories | 65

Protein | 2g

Carbohydrates |8g

Fat | 2g

Fast Snack Wraps

1 head lettuce

12 (10-inch) flour tortillas

1 (8-ounce) package cream cheese

1 (6-ounce package sliced-deli style turkey

2 cups shredded carrots

2 cups tomato, minced

> Spread cream cheese evenly over tortillas. Top with lettuce leaves. Arrange turkey slices evenly on top of the lettuce. Sprinkle tomato and carrots over turkey slices, and then roll the tortillas into wraps. Cut wraps diagonally, serve.

Cinnamon Chips and Fruit Salsa

2 kiwis, peeled and diced

2 golden delicious apples, peeled cored and diced

8 ounces raspberries

1 pound strawberries

2 tablespoons white sugar

1 tablespoon brown sugar

3 tablespoons fruit preserves, any flavor

10 (10-inch) flour tortillas

Cooking spray

2 tablespoons cinnamon sugar

> Preheat your oven to 350 degrees. In a big bowl combine the apples, kiwis, raspberries, white sugar, strawberries, brown sugar, and fruit preserves. Cover and cool in fridge for 15 minutes.

> Coat one side of every tortilla with cooking spray and cut into wedges and arrange evenly on a baking sheet. Top wedges evenly with cinnamon sugar and spray again with cooking spray. Bake in oven for 9-11 minutes and repeat with any remaining wedges. Allow to cool for 12 minutes and serve with chilled fruit mixture.

Servings | 10

Per Serving

Calories | 312

Protein | 7g

Carbohydrates | 59g

Fat | 5g

Grape and Avocado Salsa

Servings | 8

Per Serving

Calories | 66

Protein | 1g

Carbohydrates | 8g

Fat | 3g

1 ½ cups seedless red grapes, chopped

1 avocado, peeled pitted and diced

¼ cup red bell pepper, chopped

2 tablespoons yellow bell pepper, chopped

2 tablespoons sweet onion, chopped

2 tablespoons cilantro, chopped

1 tablespoon lime juice

½ teaspoon garlic salt

1 pinch black pepper

> Put the avocado, grapes, red pepper, yellow pepper, onion, cilantro in a mixing bowl. Season with garlic salt, lime juice, and black pepper. Fold the ingredients together until fully mixed. Refrigerate 30 minutes before servings.

Healthy Granola Bars

Servings | 24

Per Serving

Calories | 161

Protein | 2g

Carbohydrates | 26g

Fat | 5g

2 cups rolled oats

¾ cups packed brown sugar

½ cup wheat germ

¾ teaspoon ground cinnamon

1 cup all-purpose flour

¾ cup raisins

¾ teaspoon salt

½ cup honey

1 egg, beaten

½ cup vegetable oil

2 teaspoon vanilla extract

> Preheat your oven to 350 degrees. Grease a 9x13 baking pan. In a bowl mix together the brown sugar, oats, cinnamon, wheat germ, raisins, flour and salt. Make a well in the center and pour in the egg, honey, vanilla and oil. Mix well using your hands and pat the mixture evenly into prepared pan.

> Bake for 30-35 minutes until they turn golden around the edges. Cool for a few minutes then cut into bars while they're still warm. Make sure the bars do not cool too much before cutting or else they will turn very hard.

Spiced Sweet Roasted Red Pepper Hummus

1 (15-ounce) can Garbanzo beans, drained

1 (4-ounce) jar roasted red peppers

3 tablespoons lemon juice

Servings | 8

1 ½ tablespoons tahini

Per Serving

½ teaspoon ground cumin

Calories | 64

½ teaspoon cayenne pepper

Protein | 3g

¼ teaspoon salt

Carbohydrates |9g

1 tablespoon parsley, chopped

Fat | 2g

> Puree the red peppers, chickpeas, lemon juice, garlic, tahini, cayenne, cumin and salt in a food processor until mixture is fairly smooth. Make sure to scrape off mixture on sides of food processor in between pulses.

> Put the mixture into a serving bowl and refrigerate for 1 hour. Sprinkle the hummus with the chopped parsley before serving.

Balsamic Bruschetta

Servings | 8

Per Serving

Calories | 194

Protein | 8g

Carbohydrates | 35g

Fat | 2g

8 roma (plum) tomatoes, diced

1/3 cup basil, chopped

¼ cup parmesan cheese, shredded

2 garlic cloves, minced

1 tablespoons balsamic vinegar

1 teaspoon olive oil

¼ teaspoon kosher salt

¼ teaspoon ground black pepper

1 loaf French bread, toasted and sliced

> Toss together the basil, tomatoes, parmesan cheese and garlic inside a bowl. Mix in the balsamic vinegar, olive oil, salt and pepper.

> Serve on toasted bread slices.

Baked Kale Chips

Servings | 6

Per Serving

Calories | 58

Protein | 3g

Carbohydrates |7g

Fat | 2g

1 bunch kale

1 tablespoons olive oil

1 teaspoon salt

> Preheat your oven to 350 degrees. Put parchment paper on a baking sheet.

> Using a knife or kitchen scissors take off the leave from the stems and tear into bite sized pieces. Wash and dry the kale with a salad spinner. Drizzle the kale with olive oil and sprinkle the salt to top. Bake for about 12 minutes, or until edges are brown but not burnt.

Healthy Peanut butter Fruit Dip

Servings | 6

Per Serving

Calories |81

Protein | 4g

Carbohydrates |8g

Fat | 4g

1 (5-ounce) container vanilla Greek yogurt

2 tablespoons peanut butter

2 tablespoons honey

1/8 teaspoon ground cinnamon

2 tablespoons chia seeds (optional)

> Mix the yogurt, honey, peanut butter, and cinnamon in a bowl until fully blended. Fold in chia seeds.

DESSERT

RECIPES

Healthy Soufflé

18 ounces of hulled fresh strawberries

1/3 cup raw honey, divided

5 organic egg whites, divided

4 teaspoon fresh lemon juice

Servings | 6

Per Serving

Calories | 100

Protein | 4g

Carbohydrates | 22g

Fat | 0.5g

> Preheat your oven to 350 degrees. Put all the strawberries in a blender and pulse until fully smooth. Using a strainer, strain out the mix into a bowl and red rid of all the seeds. In the bowl of the strawberry mix add 2 egg whites, 3 tablespoons of honey, and lemon juice, beat until light and smooth. In a different bowl add remaining egg whites and beat till frothy. While beating, add remaining honey to bowl.

> Fold the egg whites into the strawberry mixture. Transfer mixture into 6 large ramekins evenly and arrange on a baking sheet. Bake for about 10-12 minutes.

Baked Rice Pudding

Servings | 8

Per Serving

Calories | 264

Protein | 6g

Carbohydrates | 49g

Fat | 4g

2 cups brown rice, cooked

2 cups unsweetened almond milk

2 large organic eggs

¼ cup raw honey

1 teaspoon lemon zest, grated

1 teaspoon cinnamon

½ teaspoon ginger

½ teaspoon cardamom

1 banana, peeled and sliced

¼ cup almond flakes

> Preheat your oven to 350 degrees and grease a baking dish. Spread out the rice evenly on the baking dish.

> In a big bowl add eggs, honey, coconut milk, lemon zest and spices and mix fully. Place this mixture over the rice, evenly. Place banana slices over egg mixture and top with almond flakes. Bake for about 20 minutes and serve warm.

Blueberry Pudding

Servings | 3

Per Serving

Calories | 53

Protein | 0.5g

Carbohydrates | 15g

Fat | 0.3g

1 small avocado, peeled, pitted and chopped

1 cup frozen blueberries

¼ teaspoon ginger, grated

1 teaspoon lime zest, grated

2 tablespoons lime juice

8-10 drops liquid stevia

5 tablespoons water

¼ cup fresh blueberries

> Add all the ingredients in a blender except for the fresh blueberries and pulse until fully smooth.

> Transfer into bowls and top with fresh blueberries to serve.

Kids Favorite Mousse

Servings | 4

Per Serving

Calories | 346

Protein | 16g

Carbohydrates | 52g

Fat | 10g

1 small avocado, peeled, pitted and chopped

1 cup frozen blueberries

¼ teaspoon ginger, grated

1 teaspoon lime zest, grated

2 tablespoons lime juice

8-10 drops liquid stevia

5 tablespoons water

¼ cup fresh blueberries

> Add all the ingredients in a blender except for the fresh blueberries and pulse until fully smooth.

> Transfer into bowls and top with fresh blueberries to serve.

.

Glazed Banana

Servings | 2

Per Serving

Calories | 145

Protein | 0.7g

Carbohydrates | 22g

Fat | 7g

1 tablespoon olive oil

1 under-riped banana, peeled and sliced

1 tablespoon filtered water

1 tablespoon raw honey

1/8 teaspoon cinnamon

1 teaspoon salt

> Heat the oil on medium heat in a non-stick skillet. Add banana slices and cook 60-90 seconds per side.

> In a bowl add the water and honey and mix well. Put the banana slices on 1 serving plate and pour the honey mixture over top. Keep aside to cool and serve with cinnamon sprinkled on top.

Instant Frozen Treat

Servings | 2

Per Serving

Calories | 202

Protein | 4g

Carbohydrates | 49g

Fat | 1g

1¼ cups fresh spinach

2 frozen ripe bananas, peeled and sliced

¾ cup frozen mango chunks

¼ cup frozen pineapple chunks

1 tablespoon unsweetened almond milk

1 teaspoon organic vanilla extract

> In a blender add all ingredients and blend until smooth and creamy, serve immediately.

Fruity Ice Cream

Servings | 2

Per Serving

Calories | 93

Protein | 2g

Carbohydrates | 23g

Fat | 1g

1 cup hulled and sliced strawberries

½ banana, peeled and sliced

2 tablespoons shredded coconut

½ cup coconut cream

1 tablespoon raw honey

1 cup crushed ice

> Put all the ingredients into a blender and blend until fully smooth. Transfer into an ice-cream maker and process according to manufacturer's directions.

> Transfer to an airtight container and freeze for 3-4 hours, stirring every 30 minutes.

70-Calorie Brownies

1 cup 70% dark chocolate chips

1 ½ cups zucchini, shredded

1 organic egg

1 cup almond butter

1/3 cup raw honey

Servings | 16

Per Serving

1 teaspoon organic vanilla extract

Calories | 70

1 teaspoon baking soda

Protein | 15g

1 teaspoon ground cinnamon

Carbohydrates | 22g

¼ teaspoon ground ginger

Fat | 6g

¼ teaspoon ground nutmeg

> Preheat your oven to 350 degrees. Grease a 9x9 inch baking dish.

> Add all the ingredients in a large bowl and mix until fully combined. Transfer the mix evenly into prepared baking dish. Use the back of a spatula to smooth out the top.

> Bake for 40-45 minutes or until a toothpick comes out clean inserted in the middle. After removing from oven let it sit a little bit to cool down. Cut into 16 squares and serve.

.

Fall Time Custard

Servings | 6

Per Serving

Calories | 130

Protein | 4g

Carbohydrates | 6g

Fat | 11g

1 cup canned pumpkin

1 teaspoon cinnamon

¼ teaspoon ground ginger

2 pinches of grated nutmeg

Pinch of salt

2 organic eggs

1 cup coconut milk

8-10 drops of liquid stevia

1 teaspoon organic vanilla extract

> Preheat your oven to 350 degrees. Mix together the pumpkin and spices in a bowl. Beat the eggs well in a different bowl. Add remaining ingredients and beat well. Add the egg mixture into the pumpkin mixture and combine fully.

> Transfer new mixture into 6 ramekins and arrange in a baking dish. Add enough water in the baking dish about 2 inches high around the ramekins. Cook for about 1 hour or until toothpick comes out clean from the middle.

Cocoa-nut Bananas

Servings | 8

Per Serving

Calories | 164

Protein | 12g

Carbohydrates | 2g

Fat | 12g

4 teaspoons cocoa powder

4 teaspoons toasted unsweetened coconut

2 small bananas, sliced on the bias

> Put the cocoa and coconut on separate plates. Roll each banana slice in the cocoa powder, and shake off any excess powder. Dip each slice in the coconut to serve.

Almond Strawberry Chia Seed Pudding

2 cups almond milk

1 (16 ounce) package strawberries, hulled

½ cup chia seeds

¼ cup honey

1 teaspoon vanilla extract

Servings | 4

Per Serving

Calories | 209

Protein | 4g

Carbohydrates | 37g

Fat | 6g

> Put the strawberries and almond milk in a blender, blend until fully smooth and then pour the mixture into a bowl.

> Stir in the honey, chia seeds, and vanilla extract into the mixture. Cover bowl and refrigerate for about 4 hours before serving.

Banana Chia Pudding

3 tablespoons honey

1 teaspoon vanilla extract

1 large banana cut in chunks

1½ cups vanilla-flavored flax milk

7 tablespoons chia seeds

1/8 teaspoon salt

Servings | 6

Per Serving

Calories | 112

Protein | 2g

Carbohydrates | 20g

Fat | 3g

>In order, put the milk, banana, chia seeds, honey, vanilla extract, and salt into a blender and blend until fully smooth.

> Put the mixture into a bowl and then refrigerate until thickened for about 2 hours, and then serve into bowls.

Mouth-Watering Fudge

2 cups chickpeas, cooked

8 Medjool dates, pitted and chopped

½ cup unsweetened almond milk

½ cup almond butter

1 teaspoon organic vanilla extract

2 tablespoons cocoa powder

¼ teaspoon ground cinnamon

Servings | 6

Per Serving

Calories | 100

Protein | 4g

Carbohydrates | 22g

Fat | 0.5g

> Cut out parchment paper onto a baking dish. Not including the cocoa and cinnamon put all ingredients into a blender and blend until fully smooth. Put the mixture into a bowl and add in the cocoa powder. Transfer this mixture onto the baking dish and spread evenly using the back of a spatula.

> Freeze for 4-5 hours or until set, and cut into squares to serve.

Blueberries with Lemon Cream

4 ounces reduced-fat cream cheese

¾ cup low-fat vanilla yogurt

1 teaspoon honey

2 teaspoons lemon zest, grated

Servings | 4

2 cups fresh blueberries

Per Serving

Calories | 144

Protein | 5g

Carbohydrates |21g

Fat | 5g

> In a bowl break up the cream cheese using a fork. Drain off any liquid from the yogurt. Add the yogurt to the bowl, as well as the honey. Use an electric mixer to beat until creamy and light, then stir in lemon zest.

> Layer the lemon cream and blueberry in either dessert wishes or wineglasses. Cover and refrigerate left over after serving.

WOULD YOU DO ME A FAVOR?

Thank you for buying my book. It is my hope that you have enjoyed the variety of recipes in this cookbook and that they aid you in your health

I have a small favor to ask. Would you take a minute to write a blurb on Amazon about this book? I look at all my reviews and love to receive feedback.

Visit the following URL to leave me a review

goo.gl/p11hsb

Also, if you have any friends or family that might enjoy this cookbook, spread the love and lend it to them!

Thank you, best wishes!

Paul

p.s. If you are interested in White Cotton Gloves for your Eczema, here are the ones I've used and they are fantastic. At the time of this writing they have over 400 positive reviews on Amazon!

www.amazon.com/dp/B018Q4WNJM?th=1

Made in the USA
Columbia, SC
10 July 2019